the

dictionary of coincidences

volume i

(hi)

s{e}an?

www.pretendgenius.com

Published simultaneously in the United States and
Great Britain in 2013 by Pretend Genius

Copyright © Sean Brijbasi

ISBN: 978-0-9852133-4-3

other books by Sean Brijbasi

One Note Symphonies
for Emma

Still Life in Motion
for those who play
Marius and Andréus

The Unknowed Things
for Julius

MATTER

for
e{m}ma+

The Tag Was Tender

An interview about my next book "the dictionary of coincidences, volume i (hi)".

Since we don't want to know the title of your next piece of shit book, what are some of the titles of your next piece of shit book that you didn't use?

The Wind, The Water, and the Wind. Bags of Potatoes. My Name is Burt. You Saw Me at the Festival of Burt in the Wind Near the Water.

Ideas are worthless and we're not really interested in where you got the idea for your dumbass book. Do you have any naked photographs of yourself that you can share with us?

I have photographs of my naked fingers I can send you. They're probably not suitable for the internet though. Not with all the cleaning up they're doing these days. I do have some of my hair and fingernails saved. I could send video of them instead of photographs. Video is more riveting.

So everyone knows genre books are for pricks. That's not a fucking question asshole.

I'm sure you are aware that genres are suitable for all age groups. If the print in books were larger I would list that as a curtain call for electric books. I've pondered the most subtle and variable effects of genre (small g) on chapter/verse themata. I remember quite vividly the lively and often raucous debates we had on the subject during my university days. Sad to think that we can't relive those times again. Ah…the wayward wanderings of a wistful meander or life as we writers like to call it.

We think a silent movie would be best for your book even though we haven't read it. So which actors do you think would be best suited to shut the fuck up on screen in a B or C movie version of your piece of shit book?

I hadn't thought about silent film. It's making a comeback is it? For silent film I would say Richard Grieco and Mario Van Peebles. Those are the two that come instantly to mind. The leading lady (if I may be so bold as to use the term) would most likely be played by Meryl Streep or Avril Lavigne.

Also, the book isn't a piece of shit sir or madam. It's a cavalcade of literary wonder. A real miracle of vision and depth. It's filled with redemption, mountain people, urban hipsters, horses, and philosophy. If you ever wanted to kill someone or yourself or not then it's a good book for reading on the weekends and for writing poems about. It's also a good book if you want to think about being entertained, enlightened, or educated.

What is a one syllable synopsis of your piece of shit book? That's as much as we're interested in.

Di.

We know this piece of shit book of yours will never be published but let's pretend for a quick second that it might be...ah fuck it...we know it never will be. What about those naked photos?

It will be published. I've sent it out to all the big small presses and a couple of the small small presses so it's just waiting to happen. I'm quite certain that one of the big small presses will publish it. But if they pass on it because it's too out there or original for them I believe one of the small small presses will take it on. And aren't naked photos cliché. Couldn't you ask for something more original? Photos of pylons for example? Far more literary and McCool as the kids like to say.

We don't like the word 'manuscript'. It's one of those bullshit words writers like to throw

around. We don't like 'work' either. We like 'piece of shit' book or 'piece of shit' story. So how long did it take you to write the first draft of your piece of shit book?

As I stated before and quite clearly I believe—it's not a piece of shit. It's a cavalcade. But it took me 17 years to finish the first draft of my piece of shit, er—I mean manuscript. I then abandoned the entire story because I had gotten too caught up in the characters. I actually thought for years that I was Mario Van Peebles. I even spoke with a German accent. I lived like that for 12, nay, 13 years before I realized that if I wanted to work in this business I had to be someone besides Mario Van Peebles. So I scrapped the first book and finished the book in its current form in 3 days. It was inspired by the first book and by my love of candles.

You fucked up writing people like to compare your piece of shit books to other books that even we reluctantly have to say aren't pieces of shit. But we don't like comparisons. We'll just leave it at that.

If I may gentle sir or madam…I would compare my book to the book based on the movie Shakespeare's Romeo and Juliet. The play is a bit too stuffy for my neo-post-classic-modern sensibilities (har har har). But I would also say it has echoes of The Robe, which is not a book but similar to a book. I think if you compared my comparisons to the comparisons of other writers you'll find that my comparisons are of a more amiable variety. Martin Amis once wrote "to compare thee to a rose would serve no purpose but to make thee roseworthy and the rose youworthy". So apt. I live by those words faithfully each day.

We don't give a rat's ass who or what inspired you to write your piece of shit book but would you like to know who inspires us? Anybody who doesn't write this piece of shit you tossed in front of us today. There are kids out there who've cured space cancer and you give us this. So we'd like you to head on down the fucking road now. Anymore of this and we'll stuff an exhaust pipe down our fucking throats while our automatic wrist slicers go to work.

Since you were candid enough to reveal your inspiration I think it's only fair that I reveal mine. It's my mum. It really is. She…I'm getting choked up here…she loves me.

We actually just killed ourselves while you were talking. You realize you've just fucking killed other human beings with your piece of shit babble about your piece of shit book. We don't give two fucks about what it's about either. So shut the fuck up and let us die in peace asshole.

It's a wartime love story about 2 men and 1 woman. There are other characters. Like Uncle Charlie who brings back jam he found in an abandoned bunker near the front lines. And Auntie Kirsten who drinks

5

a little too much because she hasn't heard from her husband in years. He disappeared during peace time and then 4 or 5 years later when the war broke out she became afraid he might have been killed in a battle and that he would never return. And the horse is a real palomino based on a real horse. I can't reveal the name. You'll try to goad it out of me. Go on you. But I won't say. Go on. I won't say no matter how much you prod me.

The Foreword Incident

I've heard there are rumours about a "Foreword Incident" concerning my unpublished book "the dictionary of coincidences, volume i (hi)" going around the internet. I would like to clear up this rumour by sharing with you the following email exchange I had with Sir Desmond Mott during the month of February. Since my last email to him I have not heard back but we are still colleagues and probably friends. While the exchange does not include exploding cars in the foreground nor erupting volcanoes in the background, it is instructive for any of you who would like forewords written for your books.

2/13/2013
Mr. Brijbasi,

I'm writing you to request that you retract the foreword I wrote for your never-to-be published book "the dictionary of coincidences, volume i (hi)". Since word leaked out that I had written the foreword, sales of my book "Death Milks the Cow" have dwindled. Furthermore, while the memory of our chance encounter brings back warm feelings, the overall memory I have of you rather disgusts me. And now I have learned that the assertions you made to me about your book were false. You said that it was a true story. Untrue. You said that you had submitted it to big publishers via your agent. Untrue. You said that it would strike a balance between the Otto Premingers of the world and the Nick Mancusos. I wasn't sure what that meant but I believed you. Furthermore, the book I wrote the foreword for was a Western adventure. So I am formally requesting that you remove the foreword and never mention our acquaintance again. Please respond to affirm that you will do so at your earliest convenience.

Respectfully,
Sir Desmond Mott

2/14/2013
Sir Desmond,

Please call me Sean. I did not writ "the dictionary of coincidences, volume i (hi)". I wrote "fraught". The tittle was later changed to "the dictionary of coincidences, volume i (hi)". The foreword you wrote therefore was for "fraught", although the manuscript you initally read was of the Western Adventure genre. I hope this clarifies the matter for you and assages your concerns. I thank you again for the foreword. Happy Valtines day.

Rejards,
Sean

2/17/2013
Mr. Brijbasi,

I don't see "wtf" *fraught* has to do with the foreword I wrote. Also, based on your mistake littered letter, I fail to see how any credible publisher would deign to make your book part of their catalogue. I am currently attending an independent publishing conference in Vermont and will not have access to email. When I return I would like to see that this matter has been taken care of to my satisfaction.

Respectfully,
Sir Desmond Mott

2/17/2013
Sir Desmond,

I want you to know that I'm working oh another book and was wondering if you could write the epilogue for that one. This book is a western and is prolly the same western you wrote the other foreword for that you thought was "fraught". I started reading "Death Miks the Cow" and I see parallels to Barthes' Y/Z and his comparison of Balzac to that other writer. Was that your intention or am I misreading your tale? Please forgiv th emistakes. I'm using my phone.

Thanks,
Sean

2/17/2013
Sir Desmond,

I think our emails were crossed. If you could reply to my first email before I respond to yours I think that would save us from confusion. I typed this on my computer.

Thanks,
Sean

2/20/2013
Mr. Brijbasi,

Barthes? Move on from your 20th century high school days sir. In any case, let me make myself absolutely clear. I will not be writing any forewords for any of your books now or in the future. I am again requesting that you remove the foreword I have written for the book that you are currently trying to get published. I would prefer not to escalate this matter but I will do whatever is legally necessary to ensure our association is severed completely and forever.

Respectfully,
Sir Desmond Mott

2/20/2013
Sir Desmond,

I assure you that I have an agent and that the book is based on a true story even though it's not a western. But you can think of it as a western that's made for modern times. And in first grade I did have an arch-enemy that I ended up having a dream about. I opened the closet and there he was. Your foreword fits because it was a coincidence that I am not publishing the book you wrote it for. So you see it fits perfectly and that's why I want to include it in my book along with the jingle written by my great-great grandfather Valdimar::ius Billimoria.

Regards,
Sean

2/25/2013
Mr. Brijbasi,

This letter serves to inform you that Sir Desmond Mott has hired counsel to deal with the foreword incident. Sir Mott has instructed us to utilize any legal measures at our disposal to ensure that you remove the foreword from your book "the dictionary of coincidences, volume i (hi)". We strongly advise you to remedy this matter to Sir Mott's satisfaction or we will pursue this matter via the courts.

Any further communication between you and Sir Mott will be conducted through his counsel.

Sincerely,
Nathanial Flantz, ESQ
Flantz, Cordero, Flantz, & Cruddup

2/27/2013
Sir Desmond,

I received a letter from a Mr. Lantz which must be a mistake. I like the foreword you wrote for my book and don't want to see it removed because some lawyer doesn't like it. I will fight this case with you. Perhaps one day we could write an account of our struggle against the bully establishment. We can't let them get away with this! Viva Zapachos!

Yours in solidarity,
Sean

They Say You Haven't Made It Until Your Mug Shot Hits The Street

Not long after the controversial Foreword Incident, I hit (as they say about addicts) rock bottom. I was reading too much. I wasn't sleeping. I was barely eating. I succumbed to the usual temptations to numb the pain. But they also say you haven't made it until your mug shot hits the street. So along with celebrities like Jim Morrison, Anthony Anderson, and Patrick Stump, I guess I've made it. But at what cost? In an effort to heal myself and help others, I am publishing the crime scene report of my recent arrest (with accompanying mug shot—certain identifying information redacted) for the public to read. To anyone who was still deciding about whether to be one of my fans or not, please forgive me.

XXXXXXXX XXXX Police Department
1707 Columbia Rd XXXXX
CRIME SCENE REPORT

CASE NUMBER: 2013-03-03-3444234-4-0-4342
INCIDENT TYPE: Disturbing the Peace
DATE: 3/3/2013
TIME: 03:14
INCIDENT LOCATION: 823 Blk 34th and K

NARRATIVE

On 3/3/2013 at approximately 0314 hours, I responded to a call on the corner of 34th and K. When I arrived, a hot dog vendor pulled me aside and pointed out the person the complaint was being made against. The hot dog vendor told me the subject, identified as Sean Brijbasi, was a regular customer on Friday and Saturday mornings after the nearby bar Fabia closed, usually around 0400 hours. Further, he stated that Brijbasi always ordered two chili dogs to go. While I was speaking with the hot dog vendor, Brijbasi—who was seated on the curb—started yelling at people crossing the street. He yelled "Kiss my ass you monkey fuckers! Poetry is dead!" He then turned to me and yelled "A is for ableberry! B is for burble!" I told Brijbasi to stop yelling. He lowered his voice and asked me if I wanted one of his chili dogs. I declined. It was obvious to me that Brijbasi was inebriated.

An adult female who introduced herself to me while I was trying to calm Brijbasi told me that before the officers arrived Brijbasi had stood on top of a car—a light blue Toronado—and recited poetry so loudly that patrons sitting at the bar's outside patio complained. Several left. Although one patron apparently made a request for something that rhymed. The female stated that she was a bartender at Fabia. Brijbasi then threw his chili dog at the female and told her to stop lying and that he had always tipped her well. He said "don't you remember the snowball fight?" The female told me that Brijbasi usually tipped well but that tonight was an exception. She said that he wasn't "acting normally" all night. I asked her what she meant by that and she told me that Brijbasi usually sat by himself at the bar without speaking to anyone but that tonight he was talking to her and laughing. I asked if he was laughing at her or with her and she stated she wasn't sure. She said Brijbasi then told her about a book deal he had just signed for 3 figures which made it even stranger about his poor tipping that night. Brijbasi then yelled out "the dictionary of coincidences you numb nuts!".

I examined the blue Toronado and saw dents on the hood. I asked Brijbasi if he had stood on the car. He told me yes but that he had been invited to stand on the car by the owner. I asked him to point out the owner to me but he told me that the owner had taken a cab home. Brijbasi then took a folded piece of paper from his pocket and handed it to me. I asked for permission to read it. He nodded. I unfolded the paper and saw a poem written on it. It was titled "fraught". I asked him if he wrote the poem and he said yes. I read the poem. I told Brijbasi that his poem was beautiful but that he should pay closer attention to his line breaks. I asked him if he had more like it. He said his book "the dictionary of coincidences, volume i (hi)" was really a book of poetry masquerading as a dictionary. I congratulated him on his book deal but he stated that he had lied to the bartender. I tried to console him by telling him that his poem reminded me of Stevens. He said he didn't like comparisons and asked me if I preferred Stevens or Williams. I said Williams. He became agitated by this and began cursing at both the female bartender and the hot dog vendor. I asked him why he preferred Stevens and he responded "fuck you bronze!" at which point I handcuffed him. He then began screaming "Night rider! Night rider!". I asked the female bartender how much he had to drink that night. She told me he doesn't drink. He just sits at the bar by himself reading. Brijbasi told me that I could keep the poem as a souvenir. I thanked him, arrested him for disturbing the peace, and drove him to the station without incident. No further information is available at this time.

Accompanying Mug Shot

Booking Number: ∞
Arrestee: Sean Brijbasi
Date: 3/3/2013

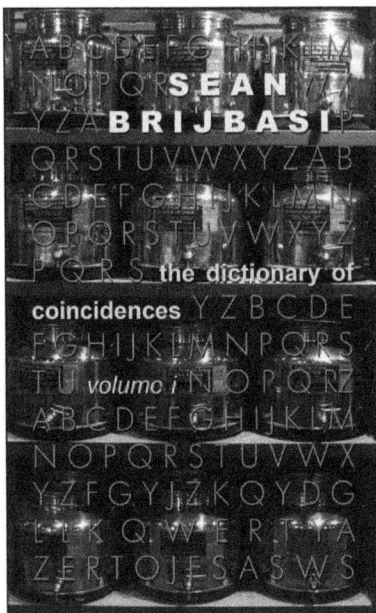

Das Book

*a poem about the book "the dictionary of
coincidences, volume i (hi)"*

the book is about nothing
the book is a fragment
of Borgia's book of sand

the book is a book about
which another unwritten
book makes reference

the story of the book

is found elsewhere

the book embraces the insignificant
part of the infinite

we may infer the book's
existence from a book
which does not exist

at the end of the book
is the start of another book

Screenplay from *the dictionary of coincidences, volume i (hi)* trailer: Unfold Freedom, Unfold (Sequence Disruptor 9)

FADE IN:

A man lying upside down on a sofa. His face is sideways(?). He has a hat on. And some cool glasses. In the background some asskick music is playing

FADE OUT:

FADE IN:

s{e}an?

At one time I thought I would just drown myself in creation. It didn't matter in which way I did it. I can't paint or sing or play any musical instruments very well. I can barely write. But barely write I do. And that is the instrument I chose to create with. I confess it was only because I wasn't good at anything else. I realized, however, that it wasn't possible to drown myself in that way. It would mean abandoning everything and everyone. It would mean forgetting about mundane but necessary activities (making money, paying bills, eating, returning phone calls). It wasn't possible for me. I had read about others doing it but it never seemed to end up well for them. I wanted to end up well. Those who make it through eventually get out of the water, so to speak. They have agents, advisers, housecleaners, accountants. But I think it becomes impossible for them to create. I think this based on sound evidence.

FADE OUT:

FADE IN:

EXT. The tops of trees passing by in slow motion (?) as if viewer is in a helicopter flying halfway above the trees and halfway in the trees.

FADE OUT:

FADE IN:

s{e}an?

At a certain point we are only replicating what was done before. Trying to return to what was once there instead of moving forward—"if only I could see the world the way I once did". Some people don't think of it in this way. They can't see it for what it is. They don't see what prevents them from drowning. Every piece of instruction is a life vest. Every insight not gained through experience is a buoy. Every 'it must be so' is floating debris one clings to. Every longing to recapture what one once possessed prevents one from going deeper. We prevent ourselves from going deeper. We are kept afloat. But these things may also have value. They show us how deep the sea is—they reveal the boundaries across where we can clearly see the peril. In time, if we think of it in the right way—

and this is especially difficult to do—all of this may become part of the experience—part of the weight—that sinks us deeper.

FADE OUT:

FADE IN:

EXT. More tops of trees passing by as if viewer is in a helicopter flying halfway above the trees and halfway in the trees.

FADE OUT:

FADE IN:

Dodo

Gigi

FADE OUT:

FADE IN:

Gigi

Dodo

FADE OUT:

FADE IN:

s{e}an?

Naturally there were experiences that produced the content of my first book "One Note Symphonies". But they weren't distinct experiences. It was never a case where one incident became the axis around which a story revolved. My memory has always been vague and so my memories became blurred. I remember myself in situations that could not have possibly occurred. I misplace people. I misplace locations. From this misplacement new situations and images are created. I think this is quite normal.

FADE OUT:

FADE IN:

INT. A desk drawer is opened. We see a hand take a silver 9mm gun out of a drawer. The gun is pointed toward the floor.

FADE OUT:

FADE IN:

s{e}an?

I have no memory of "Still Life in Motion".

FADE OUT:

FADE IN:

INT. Someone is walking quietly up the stairs. We don't see who it is. It's creepy.

FADE OUT:

FADE IN:

s{e}an?

From "The Unknowed Things" I can infer the machinations behind "Still Life in Motion". If I think of my work as a progression, an evolution, a Hegelian "unfolding of freedom" (as I would like to think of it) then "The Unknowed Things" was the work that provided the clearest example of this unfolding. "Still Life in Motion" then must have been a counter-lever to the necessary improvement of my memory. Memory which is itself anathema to the unfolding but without which survival is impossible. And perhaps that is why I have no memory of "Still Life in Motion". "The Dictionary of Coincidences" then is the apotheosis of this progression. My progression. After this, I think there can be no more and certainly no less.

FADE OUT:

FADE IN:

INT. A closed door. A hand reaches out to open it. Turns the doorknob. Black. Opens the door. We see the gun from behind. Someone is holding it.

The person moves into the room. Raises the gun and points it.

FADE OUT:

FADE IN:

s{e}an?

I was and am still happy.

FADE OUT:

FADE IN:

INT. The trigger of the gun is pulled. We hear the sound of the shot. The gun kicks back in the shooter's hand. We see the book "the dictionary of coincidences, volume i (hi)" on a bed (sleeping?) with a hole in it—shot and bleeding. Spinning spinning spinning. Dying dying dying.

FADE OUT:

Biografetus

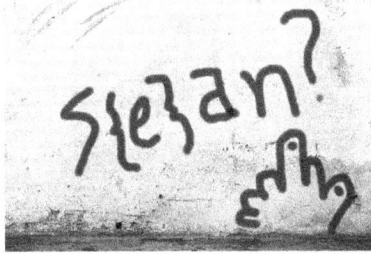

Near Potsdamer Ponz. Berliner Starstation. *the dictionary of coincidences, volume i (hi)* author tags Europe (name changed to preserve artificial habitat of location). This was the very first place that my tag appeared ever in the world. In existence. In America the tag first appeared at the top of the Washington Monument in Washington D.C. With the help of local resistors I was able to scale the smooth, cool marble and leave my mark for a sleepy nation to see. Wake up nation!

After the tag was reported to authorities, a government agency simulated an earthquake in D.C. and its surrounding areas. The monument was then closed to visitors while 'repairs' were being made. Nevertheless, in an act of unprecedented defiance, I visited the following day.

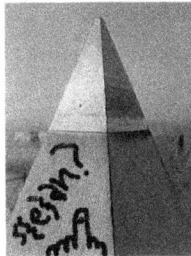

In the picture below you'll see workers preparing to remove my tag from outside the Sistine Chapel's conclave room at the Vatican. It looks pretty darn good. The following week I received a letter from a cardinal so-and-so with the church's imprimatur regarding my book *the dictionary of coincidences, volume i (hi)* so long as I refrained from tagging anywhere on Vatican grounds in the future. I framed the imprimatur to add to my imprimatur collection and tagged the door of the Poste Vaticane in light pencil the following day.

In Sweden I tagged ancient runes. The child in the picture below is mesmerized by my symbols of fascination. It was a moving experience for me to add my imprint to those of people who lived thousands and hundreds of years ago. I live now. I took this picture pretending to be a tourist from China. Don't forget me Sweden!

It's important to remember that these tags are not signifiers. They are instead what is signified by *the dictionary of coincidences, volume i (hi)*. The relationship between the signifier and the signified in this case is purely coincidental. The book was published based solely on this "what is signified" without so much as a hint of what the signifier might be. The publisher never read the manuscript. Am I lucky or what?

My Collection of Large Nurses

An elephant is large but not compared to the universe. So when I say I have a collection of large nurses I mean large compared to a stick of dynamite. A small nurse is good but a nurse larger than a stick of dynamite is also good.

Harald, my first large nurse, specialized in nutrition. He tried to cure me of eating food with my hands. While this had societal benefits I didn't feel that it benefited me in any way. I still continued to eat food with my hands when it suited me. Harald really wasn't of any use to me but I found that I couldn't part with him.

It wasn't that I had become emotionally attached to him; it was just that the thought of letting him go overwhelmed me with the feeling that to let him go would trigger some existential crisis that presaged the start of my ontological unraveling. So I kept him.

The second nurse I collected (Philomena) was larger than Harald but she was very light on her feet. I could hardly hear her around the house, which pleased me. She prescribed dill weed to me for my bouts of breath-shortness. We also watched films together while Harald studied his music. Philomena's favorite film was *Invasion of the Body Snatchers*, although we watched the occasional sports film from time to time. She didn't mind crying and sometimes bawled effusively at the slightest perceived sadness. But she never laughed even when I used my greatest jokes on her.

I continued collecting large nurses—sometimes two at a time—whenever and wherever I could find them. I had a large nurse in my collection who was an expert gardener (fresher dill weed). I had another large nurse who could spackle like a born handyman (useful but ultimately uninspiring).

It wasn't until I found Maria that my craving for large nurses ended. Maria was the 23rd large nurse I had collected—the large nurse that was the pinnacle of large nurses. The *sui generis*, the *Ṣalāḥ al-Dīn Yūsuf ibn Ayyūb*, the *Queen Regent*…

My collection of large nurses can walk single file between the spaces of parked cars.

Maria was a pediatric nurse—meaning she nursed small children. She wasn't sure what to do about me as I wasn't a small child so instead of nursing me she read to me before I fell asleep. After the second night of her reading to me I realized that what I had really been looking for while I was collecting large nurses was a dictionary. I asked Maria if she had a dictionary that she could read to me (she didn't). Or if she knew someone who had a dictionary that she could read to me (again she didn't). She listed the alphabet out for me randomly instead and advised me to doodle words that correlated to each letter. That was her prescription? I asked for a diagnosis (things had started to proceed quickly) and she diagnosed *inertia*.

Should I doodle *inertia*? Was that her way of dialectically medicating me? But I didn't doodle *inertia*.   Instead   I   doodled *industrial-machinery*. I asked her if this was her doing but she said that I alone was responsible for my response to *inertia* and for the first time in months I didn't think about watching sports films and/or Philomena.

I   went   on   a   doodle   frenzy.   I doodled *ableberry*. *Zebra-horse*. *Chromosome*. *Hide-you-place*. I was ebullient (whatever that means). *Burble*. *Jespertine*. I was all powerful (I was overcome by a feeling of power). I foreheard the country foghorn before the deep muuuuuur came and emptied all thought from my brain.

When the foghorn waned my thoughts came back to me and I asked Maria to record my words exactly as I said them to her in some manner that she was good at. She was good at italics.

"I'm a jingle writer…"

The Foreword

There is little if anything profound about 'the dictionary of coincidences, volume i (hi)'. It is only appearance. Written in a style more reminiscent of Ribera's Pointilism[i] and yet, because of its systematic approach, somewhat apart from those haphazard techniques. The work asks no great questions (nor even small ones). It provides no great answers (nor even small ones). Its author performs neither the work of the novelist nor of the poet. Despite its best effort to organize whatever it is attempting to organize in order to bring order to the chaos of its own existence, there is no truth to be found in its pages, no discovery of only what the work itself can discover. It is a life impervious to external examination. It provides no mirror. It informs only itself.

Sir De(s)mon-d Mott, author of Death Milks the Cow

The Prologue

I'm a jingle writer
My relative was Purdy
When you need that shine
And think "hmm that's absurd", he
Wrote about coincidences
From a boat that wasn't sturdy
I'm a jingle writer
My relative was Purdy

--*Valdemari::us Billimoria*

A

ableberry

*and lo there goes my father [she's singing] stop
staring. irretrievable the floor vanished. and for
only me {she} carried my body to the strafe.*

Underneath the glass she looks the same but her
hair is different. I remember the smell of her room
and the window barely opened looking down onto
the small yard and how the breeze lifted her
drawings from the wall. When she returned I would
hear her bicycle rattle against the tree, the front
door open and close, and her hurried footsteps
getting nearer to our room. I always thought to
myself and sometimes whispered: 'be careful on the
stairs'. That's how much I loved her.

amputake

*let's not talk of skeletons while we [together] we
[alone] are here. Upstairs at Be^lla's I outlined the
future and jotted you down with fine penmanship
while staring at pictures of hair and honey or what
I thought of then as insertion.*

We are lonely moving near the place of our
surrender. Coming and then replacing real life
jumping. The girl and the girl in the kilt stove.
Breathing a mop of wood, flake, and sordid
collapse.

41

She bells the intense coma of slinging. A pastor of disruption and friendly marbles living. Her upright girdle splendor splinters the ram's nest. Blink darling (blink). The pied-*à*-terre amalgam of rooster.

Her name is Jeffam|a|r and she purports to be unsung. Screeds of two laps curtailing the axiom of vanish*ment*.

andventures of the cornbread maker

divide the reich and press our interests in the north.

Renumber the planets and bring them lovely. Hi//rosito Kamasas!hi is a comic book fighter. Oolong Hi//rosito. Lumps of plum and dilly.

B

bend human willing

i lay awake during their nights, thinking of their deaths, regretting how i made so many of their kind suffer and how i should die of pity and regret if it were not for this jawbone and iron belly.

The existence of the phantom is subtlety. He is posh and exerts his fisticuffs without clumsy. He is whimsy. He courts ladies of leisure for the touch of velveteen on their bottoms. It is a copious matter. He adorns them with lather.

burble

picture me in time when I reigned in this loci. It is the east, and she is the sun. But how now dear she? A rat. Dead for a ducat. And you, masturbating to the vicar's memory.

There were three decided. Finally and unearthed. The Spenserian Model[ii] and the luhkow. Bath to bath she balanced tea on her mandible tongue. When the prawns and mercenary scabbards came to shave her of her purpose she protested to fracture go when. This was an introduction to her brow and down beneath. The poke stick hint of her shanty, her eye blood swelling in a puddle of rain, and the pork stench of her hollow. I followed her through the recoil [a french disaster] and consoled her of a time not too long ago when the presence of mercury suggested fossil degeneration and of men later revealed as Hermione fainting on the beach.

At night she lay on a cold bed with me and through a roofless hut watched mandarin leaves travel through the jet stream. So different from the time of Hammerstein of the Volstein, Royal Chrysanthemum of the Haubsfelt.

But as if on a living she modified her thinking with a reckon and showed me the door. And though it was not to my liking I set off for out there but feared I would return one day to gather mud from this place and find pieces of her in my hand. She ate well (sir) but what good was such good when it only prolonged her bad? Die I whispered from the horizon. Die for your own quiet deathness. But she lived on. Were she an animal, they would call her human.

C

caroma sink

the windows and doors of her steamy southern plantation house. A rare draft. The sticky bodies of her slaves.

The day was pictures. And no words neither because of the dark. Lifting companions on the voice of a single finch. A corporal dissension among the hierarchy club. Here where we walk subdued and circle, maybe in yes.

chinese and uninvolved

we think of warsaw and the wall and the measly five marks it would cost to stop that moaning in the dark, if only we were allowed to pay.

She often wondered how it felt to walk across a street and see men and women unable to take their eyes off of her. But it never happened. She drifted in streams beneath them. She felt that she had beauty in her and sometimes so much so that she would forget what she looked like. She'd think to herself that her beauty was escaping to the surface and that people could see it, like when she thought about rain or ducklings drifting on a calm lake. She watched to see if eyes turned to her when she felt this way but she was never sure. Maybe it was just the luck of the draw that her beauty was hidden. But then she'd think it didn't have anything to do with luck or fate or destiny because only those two people who made her could have made her and only at that very moment in time, and that if she hadn't been made then, then she would have never been made. So she accepted the fact that she couldn't have been anyone else but who she was at that very moment. Ever.

chromosome

the trail simmers cold in this hollow sleepy town

This is what they describe to you while the Martinique revolution plucks the roots of her lightly moistened wheat fields. There is a pause and then it continues. She harbors a sleight predilection for plaster. Three times the weight of heavy. Horn made of Punjabi silk. Enough a) to make one festoon. And rightly so. For the compromise dissembles her bungalow. Soft width pillows and shams, designed for maximum comfort. Oh Maria, how little the time ticks when dressed in stripes and plastic blaster spoons.

They say trees grow in her sitting room.

She warns me that (uh) here come the stupid words again. And they're all (all) around again. And I read (read) them again. And nothing (nada) new again. Same old partitions and eyeglass suck. And she's right as a bauble in that come with me (so I fondle her) way.

Through the phonoplane to the pigeon house where they give words to everything. Even silence and nothing and bob who is nameless. Oh yes, Math-i-lda, the boo-hoo makes her sad. But I pop wheelies and hammer her nipples into a smooth child-like fluffy.

Presently she sips tea beneath palm leaves and makes pronouncements as bare as winter while mangos sweat in the bowl beside her. Lately I've been meaning to tell her something along the lines of a parable. But after a deflection of her existence and in spite of distractions, it seems she'll never let me go. And I should love her as one might love a mother but the Roman in me finds fault in even love.

Oh unbridled mare of Tunisia, Sierra Leone and Monjolia, etc., etc...

She laments that nothing ever happened to her that was big enough to connect the world {the whole Nicaragua bullshit and fucked up alcoholic and tangerines like pornographic bible verse}.

To say to someone: this is what happened to me under the awning while planes fired overhead.

To say to someone: they once made jam that looked like candle wax and sent it by boat to barely remembered outposts and that one time (one time dear C*letus) I jarred a note that read: *come back for me.*

"These things happen to prevent one from floating away and I have no stories to tell."

All of her responses, impersonations—she loves hemoglobin for what it's worth. A pressing sensation of Thrasym+achus the conniver, the iron made collapser, encircling her residue, cubing her— not what you're thinking—porpoise flail.

Tell your stories first and then live them, you stupid girl.

But she's no stupid girl when she leads you by the hand and plunges you pinky first into her Hammurabi wigwam. Je{su}s Chri:st, she's got pudding down there.

But you're never alone 'cause it's never allowed. Even sitting beneath the palm trees that grow through her roof like leafy plugwig and scrubby and her head caught in your lap as the warm, night breeze calms her to sleep, you hear the crowd mumble {chromosome}. A drone in the pontiff's ear. A stream of blood like a locust swarm.

SEQUENCE DISRUPTOR 1

dear s{e}an?,

i feel inspired by a more than capable comrade (who has written observations on poets and poetry titled 'how to be a poet, for idiots.') to issue forth observations on gooder writing. i have from time to time been known to offer something or other to those who seek it. not all of this something or other is understandable, however, and based on the cloistered nature of the human brain (meaning yours) this is not surprising. but due to my philoprogenitive nature i rise above the tendency of most 'writers' to horde and shall therefore generously particularize the monads of gooder writing for you (always for you) in this letter.

i. addressing the fundamental flaws in your approach

- the notion that gooder writing can be learned is false.
- the notion that reading can help you become a gooder writer is false.
- the notion that 'workshopping' can make you a gooder writer is false.
- the notion that feelings (suffering, love, happiness, grief, the 'heart') is the birthplace of gooder writing is false.
- the notion that the telling of a good story comprises gooder writing is false.

- the notion that mastery of language produces gooder writing is false.

if you believe that any of these notions have helped you to become a gooder writer, i assure you the connection (perceived) is coincidental. in short, everything you have thus far believed as it relates to gooder writing is false. once you have purged your quill of these dumbass beliefs, you will be ready to work on your bow.

ii. observation is what goes in, it's something else entirely that comes out

were you a gooder writer this would be perfectly clear to you. but since you are not i shall make it crystal clear.

what one observes should not also be what one relates. a blue bird, for example, once recorded by the brain, should not then be preserved by that brain for the purpose of recitation. the recordation of the blue bird should serve as a template that will become sublimated, transformed, coalesced (with x), enhanced. i shall call this the 'alchemization' of the blue bird. this, like observation, is an involuntary reflex of the limited human brain that requires little of its already teenie-weenie functional capacities.

should someone observe a blue bird only to recite 'blue bird' or 'flying blue thing with some other sharp pointy thing on its head' we can say that what that someone is reciting is the original recordation of the blue bird which served as the brain's template. this is non-fiction/journalism crap and does not comprise gooder writing. The alchemization of the blue bird, although complete, is inaccessible to this someone (you).

iii. the two necessary events following alchemization that bring about the effect known as gooder writing

although the involuntary alchemization of what one observes provides the stuff of gooder writing, the ability to access this stuff without de-alchemizing it or un-transforming it is what separates gooder 'writers' from less gooder 'writers'. it is therefore necessary that two events occur following alchemization:

1. the destruction of the original recordation that served as the template from which the alchemization occurred.

the destruction of the original template launches the mind into a realm known to you as the 'imagination'. the destruction of this template can also be called 'letting go'. i'll note for you, although it should be obvious, that the 'letting go' does not occur prior to the alchemization, nor is the 'letting go' necessary for the alchemization to occur. the letting go or destruction of the original template facilitates the accessing of the alchemization from the area the alchemization occurred (the "imagination"). should the original template not be completely destroyed, the effects produced would be similar to *dada* or *beat* as the mind is still hanging by one arm, so to speak, from the partially undestroyed original template. the mind, in turn, wanting to let go but not having the courage to completely let go produces writing based on this awareness, which resembles something that may have been the effect of this 'letting go' but in reality is an effect produced by wanting to let go, being afraid to let go, not wanting anyone to know you are afraid to let go, and finally not being able to let go. this is not gooder writing.

what more, 'letting go' artificially by some external means is also evidence of the lack of courage necessary to let go. this also depreciates the original template, for even though the original template must be destroyed, seeing it *as it is* is vital to its alchemization. this type of artificial letting go also produces royal crapola.

the destruction ('letting go') of the original recordation that served as the template from which the alchemization occurred is the most difficult and important part of gooder writing. should one not destroy the original recordation or 'let go', the ability to access the alchemized blue bird in the 'imagination' is impossible. it may seem like a simple thing to do but i assure you that less than 1% of 1% of the entire human population, present and past, has ever had the ability to 'let go' for the purpose of producing gooder writing.

2. the accessing of the alchemization of the original recordation.

once one has 'let go', the ability to access the alchemization of the original recordation is academic. it is not a matter of how this accessing occurs, just as it is not a matter of how one gets wet in the ocean. it simply occurs.

it is my desire that this letter lays bare for you the futility of attempting gooder writing and that you abandon all hope of achieving it. if however, you continue in your pursuit despite my warning, a more nuanced elaboration of this letter shall follow.

yours in sympathy,
e{m}ma+ gla::s

D

darker circles of her body

cue remember

Undress and stretch. Your arms and legs to the sun.

dreams of terrible angels

two lovers in the snow. Two lovers framed by jade (color). Two lovers pierced by the sword of a mighty rhododendron (flower).

Ros|e-mary. The gentles call to you from Hibiscus. The bare settles in. The cardinal falls through the ice—his mitre a maypole for more graceful children, who having filled their cheer with scrawn, live artfully among the mundane.
Stricken with night, the dog breaks its own leg and vomits the stars before us.
I can't remember the songs. Only the women who sang them and the ground they stood on. The bluster of hair as clouds moved behind them. Praying to the old logic. We who are human never wanted the necessity. The looking up in shock. The inevitable coming to this of life. When she died I followed her to the door and held her face in my wound. They say there will be more for those who are beautiful.

In our pain, we can split with old times, always breathe so logical new times. We can look there though it's different—in the universe where the dust in which gods sleep, soak up the blood of good men—in our pain there, though it's different, we can split with new times, always breathe so comical near times.

And in a jar in a place more real than the world, we saved her last breath and imagined the molecules of her lungs building a world of their own. We remember how her mouth twisted and how she fell to her knees and tried to sit in a way that only she knew, one more time to be reassured that this strangest of feelings would not be her last.

The compassion of Seneca and the kindness of noble men are spit. A dying body flails and settles on itself. The old widows know this.

I once kissed Ros|e-mary on her earlobe, that piece of skin too small for love. But I destroyed it with love. I sat on the chair beside her. I heard footsteps on the grass outside. I placed my lips on her ear. The wind blew sheets of music onto the floor—*ballade, saisir, sonata a due*. She leaned down to pick them up and whispered something into her own mouth.

Darkness never came for anyone as light as she. The guardians of the soul of hell. The tight bandage of hell where wisdom sustained only itself while we descended into the lurch of dog and pig and the excess of discharge.

Ros|e-mary played for me as I left. Each moment I turned to watch, she placed her hands on her lap. I heard the music behind me as I closed the door.

We thought we were too old to be trapped inside of ourselves. That too many dull blades had left their mark and revealed what was at bottom. But at bottom, we still had enough strength to hide, to move away, to think better of saying it—the one thing that would have made everything different between us.

Ros|e-mary exhaled for the last time the word she whispered into her own mouth: *life*. All of it. Every piece. Even the waste and the vile and the hate that infected both sides of her skin. But when she was young her body trembled with what it was to be beautiful—when we wanted to forever have her in that moment before we did.

E

european sciences

i raise the cutlass i hold in my hand.

In modern day Europe one observes a crisis of American proportions. The sub-valleys and tinkers, swathed in their own egress, migrate like flan against the ever-fluid Tiber. On either side one sees abandoned stalls. The sun over this epoch shimmers in the way nets of dying fish do. A period of long twilight awaits man. A time of deep and revealing sleep. Fish will rot and die, their fossils providing a thousand blueprints for the evolution of a far greater and noble breed. The basic sub-structure of the current dilemma is the culmination of an evolutionary conflict between the pre-*a priori* process of the conscience (synaptic cross-lattice burbling) and the 'resultant' of this conflict (phonoplane deceleration). Although one appears to follow the other, a causal relationship between the pre-*a priori* process and phonoplane deceleration cannot be determined.

evil of goodness

this dream-like sequence, the basis of all conversation, is an example of a near-perfect combination of form and function. It provides an environment in which people can exist [live]. Rules are established of what can or should be said and of what cannot or should not be said. In turn, expectations are met, practice is rewarded, and humans may interact in relative safety.

We're on a ship that's sinking and you and I move away from where the water's filling. They'll bring a fire truck on deck to put out the fire. It's a long ship and there's lots of space. But we'll have to jump over. Near the ship there's a pond and we see pond things while we're swimming underneath. Storybook pond things that invert words like vespertine (from the viny) or crepuscular just for this sense. It looks like an old city but it's just an old town. And when the Indian sailors come rowing over to tell us how they fixed her up, we'll tell them to row back because we'll be staying here a while. We'll say 'you'll find us waiting here M+ati/lda, our sweat collecting in the creases of a bamboo porch.'

It could be the land of turtles or the land of underneath water. But we are a relevant species, scraping chum along the briny, humming jingles while flowers bloom from the bottom of our shoes.

F

feeltrip

what mendacity is this that proclaimed itself thus upon my bereavement? It is a cold bluster of mind that turns to keep a man's soul from ascent.

This is the way of Marstrand[iii]—passing five sins to Marga^re|t. She is of consequence in her plastic arcade. Some whisper in search of favorite colors and numbers and I am that boy. Someone made the cave. Someone made the footpath to the slave. Someone made the slave. It was all still and then she flew. In the cave pictures of new animals (they say *we were almost apart*).

There is a noise that reminds me of my loss. Those missing on the ferry to Marstrand. The walk by the water and rocks. The *fell*. My loss saved in half bubbles floating in puddles of rain. The boats painted [yellow and blue] with ropes drifting out to the boy.

I am entering now. The place. The skin beneath her skin that I touch (more than touch, more than skin) in the room above the sea where the bones of men mingle with those of animals.

SEQUENCE DISRUPTOR 2

dear ms. gla::s,

   i thank you for your letter and commend your fancy thoughts. i commend them in spirit and, in good time, i applaud your comrade for his observations on poetry for poetry is the architect of all things possible (and therefore impossible) as well as the impetus for the ribonucleic acids. i offer as proof of my heartfelt soliloquy in response to your effective reasoning, *submatter* D-G.

   i consider it the only retort worthy of contemplation. so let us be contemplative but wary of the somnolent tones of academia. hmmmmm.

slippy yours,
s{e}an?

G

god 17 (she)

i never want you to die.

In the hallways of the Barium League[iv] he spoke to her of nuclear-prosthetic vision and the phenomena of amino-wave patterns that subjects saw during his experiments but he couldn't remember her name. He had seen her on the bus earlier in the afternoon, sitting three rows over to his right. He tried to imagine her thought processes when she rubbed herself with soapy water in the shower. He liked her breasts. He liked the brains of them.

grabben

one desires meanli to settle into one's chest like pollen. Or sanding [my brother poomsi] threw Alabama wood like the porch we sat on because [sometimes] people who are at home fall and die and [sometimes] people who are not at home fall and die.

On your ear he said, so fervent and nubile in his enthusiasm, a quasi-liturgical membrane strutting from his turnip hut. Some whispered his sociopathy, others his relegation to the mutter fields, while après mort lay sidewise and pressed their blood cabbage to the ground.

There is lip everywhere. And nose. And strump.

In the doorknob summer comes early but out here all is gray while Hiroshima father breastlespur consumes himself. His twin bourbons metastasized with youthy flailings. Oh swine but singworthy messenger. Trinkets flea like big, materializing in astonishment cymbals for the martyr. On friar purr day, the protozoa march in wiggly [wait for me oh she!], in her summer clover and glistening lips of sardine (punctuation for a whisper)

H

hide-you place

we heard his grandfather in the background mumbling something about the Germans. His mother couldn't bring herself to speak. His father said he liked to invent new words and pretend that he could only see out of one eye.

She wanders in like a person, fumbling and graceless. I have her shoes. She's come to fetch them and take them down the road to put in the last phone booth in town to see if anybody's going to walk off with them. She watches from the bus stop where bus after bus drives by before she gets fed up. But nobody uses the phone so she grabs her shoes and brings them back to my place.

I don't know anybody in this town. Ain't got no lads on the corner. Or a Sa#lly come by for the occasional and proper. Just her. Fumbling and graceless. Coming and going for her shoes. I don't even know her name and after a time I don't want to. In my mind I call her Ali:c:e. She doesn't look like an Ali:c:e but after a few weeks she grows into Ali:c:e. Now I'm afraid she's a Ja!net or a Carl+{a. Not that there's anything wrong with Ja!nets and Carl+{as but I've grown into Ali:c:e too. So I don't ask her.

She calls me 'man'. Hey 'man'. I come to get my shoes 'man'. Getting a drink 'man'. The word sounds young in her mouth. Like she's practicing. I

67

don't call her anything. I just say 'sure'. Or 'yeah'. Or 'go on'. I sometimes wonder if I care about her—that if one day she doesn't show up I would worry that something happened to her. Yeah, I probably would. But I don't feel like I'd be able to do anything about it.

She goes to the sink and drinks straight from the faucet. She doesn't ask anymore. After she leaves I drink straight from the faucet too, worried she'll walk back in and catch me, and I'm overcome by a feeling of disapproval because I think people—people who don't drink straight from faucets—would see something vulgar in it. There might be.

haze factory

quite dapper my good man. Years if not days swing in my musky playground. A pipe sitdown by the—draw close—fire. Raaaar. Don't get boined.

I remember the summers and the sun during this time. The light from above. The iron gates and wooden benches. And you and him. How happy as the tree behind you shimmered. He picked you up and you held around him. Why couldn't you be mine? I am older here. I can imagine the feeling. To hold this type of beauty. To pick you up and pull you into my chest. Maybe you argued. Maybe it wouldn't last. But not at this moment. This moment that was yours was always around me.

What is Paris? Or Berlin? Or Athens? From up there it is the tower, the wall, the acropolis. Down here it is the small apartment, the water in the street, the voice of a friend calling behind you when you have gone outside to be sick. Even Moscow with all of its plumage returns to the small flat I grew up in where I knock on the door and the girl who is still drinking her milk listens from the other side and the boy brushing his teeth peeks through the window.

I

industrial machinery

*lift play and swing the plastic army boys lost
beneath the bed [underneath] and the pattern of the
rug frilled at the edges lifted to find coins and
chocolate wrappers and the glorious window—tree
half-hanging and steeped in navigation.*

I think about walking and meeting people who
want to talk to me. Who. Who stop me and ask me
questions about nothing. In a park or adjacent to a
park. Someone sitting on a bench while kids fidget
in school where teachers talk about nothing.

"Your skin is very dark and pale", you say.

I move closer. You had a girlfriend you were
seeing and she made you very happy. The breeze is
light and the leaves crinkle under our behaviour.
How did she sleep? I touch your hair. Yesterday I
slept on my side and thought about legumes I
planted in a hidden plot near the train station. Two
little legumes grew but I was anxious and plucked
them before they were ripe. I spy them under my
coat when no one is looking.

"I don't like the sun", you say.

There's no texture in the grass here. It's too
smooth. Almost like paper that's coloured green.
And the sky is the same. The sun looks like the
face of a child that a child has drawn but I don't
stare because of photosynthesis. There are
paintings of cannibals in the museum. Strange

71

women with postures of gold and Persephone tincture ranging down on servings of humanity.

"I want to go somewhere with you and fall asleep", you say.

We hold hands. You comment on the innovation of my fingers. Their slender precision. I tell you that my sleep is appealing—like the space between two branches of a tree. It breathes. The air flows through and around my sleep. Like a ballerina around a perfect éphémère. If you walk beside my sleep you will feel it on your face. Something changes around me—the consistency and hue of the air that navigates my musculature.

"We can go to where my bed is and sleep", I say.

You hear the sound of a blanket on the clothesline. Dogs appear from the dust and run through the opened space.

"I just want to be quiet for a time", you say. "There's too much noise and without saying it."

There is enough time for all the wrongs in this world. Even ours. But ours is freakish and slit with rungs and the pounding of Ga:-lileo. They spit everywhere and hate us for collecting their bile. But my room is clean today. The walls have been pampered with loving and the floor by my bed cozied with and snuggled.

"You have many books", you say.

"Yes I have many books in my room, most of which I haven't read but of those I haven't read my favourite is *Notes from Underground* given to me by an uncle who thought it time for me to broaden my horizons. I was, but no longer am, a country girl in dress and temperament. And he, in his way, had hopes of improving my lexis while I had hopes of gaining insight into the ways of the world. The book has been well kept despite its discolouration. And though it is a paperback, the spine is sturdy and bells a convincing tone when tapped against the edge of a table. I suspect the story takes place in a sewer with a single manhole that one cannot open but can see through to the outside world. I believe it to be a metaphor for the human soul."

You circle the room then settle onto the bed upon which we hope to cultivate our loneliness. We hear the sound of iron and stone. Children who search for trinkets near the factory make piles of chrome. They hold up pieces of broken glass to the sun.

SEQUENCE DISRUPTOR 3

dear s{e}an?,

there is a burden that beauty places upon us. it requires that we act, that we become, and that we are always becoming. but you do nothing but offer these misgivings and let your tender neckline suffer from the cold. D-E has already caused the untimely death of my pup and i cannot read on. you ask me to cue remember but your *submatters* are up to no good. still, i know in my heart that my journey to the pretty dress store will be plentiful with honour and transcendence even without the frisky companionship of my dear Pene[l]ope. i wonder whence your malice arose.

D-E reminds me of Cho+pi{n}, though not in the right way. i cannot be certain you know of the legend so i will relate it to you as only one who has great concern for you can so that you might learn from he who was far greater than you.

in September 1849, a few weeks before he died Cho+pi{n} wrote a small pamphlet on the existence of a note he believed he had accidentally discovered while playing for an audience at the residence of Lady Gain;sbor;ough. another noise, the origin of which he could not determine, 'crossed the path' of his nocturne and ever so briefly produced a note he had never heard before. he called this note the *transnote*. i believe you are searching for such a "note". the pamphlet has never been found and there is reason to believe that Cho+pi{n}'s sister destroyed it along with some of his lesser works at his request. however, anecdotal evidence exists that support its purported contents.

for one, following the discovery of the *transnote* Cho+pi{n} became increasingly concerned about the distance between himself and his audience. he wanted the distance to be no more and no less than the distance between himself and the audience at Lady Gain;sbor;ough's. while Cho+pi{n}'s concern for this distance was excessive, i strongly recommend that you consider this distance between you and your audience in order to avoid the mistakes of D-E if, despite my advice to the contrary, you decide to continue with this strange *obsession* of yours.

Delacr*oix- mentions Cho+pi{n}'s sudden fixation in letters he wrote to his brother. prior to the Gain;sbo;rough concert, no such concern on Cho+pi{n}'s part is documented. Cho+pi{n}'s frustration at not finding this note may also have led him to destroy several pianos in what witnesses described as an 'ungodly fit of rage', behavior in stark contrast to his reserved and quiet reputation. one wonders if you are creating in such a rage?

but my concern is not only for the guilty. it is for the innocent as well for Jen!!ny Lin*d described how on several occasions while visiting Cho+pi{n} during the last year of his life, he would mumble in his sleep 'i must find it, i must find it' over and over again until, mid-mumble, he became quiet and fell asleep for good.

i implore you to heed my loving advice. nothing will cross the path of your words to create what you are seeking and if such a singular event

ever did occur, i assure you, that like Cho+pi{n},
you will go to your grave searching but never
finding.

i show you my leg,
e{m}ma+ gla::s

J

jeller

*good soldiers we were when the time came to swim
irish or (mhm), a free frolic oratorium, a tooth two
teeth for private recrimination. The tree [bulbous]
brought giddy and set two lumps afire and flung
them far into the megalosphere.*

Her pain went unrecognized by the authorities so
she began the process of making her pain official,
gathering all of the official documents and
applications, organizing them into folders that she
kept on her bedside table. She filled in her personal
information, all of the places she had ever lived,
places she had been on holidays. She was so
thorough that she managed to pinpoint through her
examination the exact date on which her pain
began.

Documenting her pain filled her with an
optimism that she had rarely experienced until she
read the admonition concerning witness testimony
in the fine print of one of the many applications.
Did her witnesses know that she was in pain? Did
they see her in pain? They would be interviewed to
make certain. False or incomplete witness testimony
brought a harsh penalty and perhaps more pain. But
she had never told anyone about her pain and
therefore abandoned all hope of it ever being
recognized.

jespertine

gone good are days of long and lonely suffering when the window shingles (fermata, algernon, and caribou) conspire with words like reckon or dragoon master willister to confound us.

Ours was the house seen from the road. But only the back door and the bedroom window above, framed by trees on either side. If you had a pretty dress mother or one moment to rest upon the stairs I would have told you that not far from here I impressed a girl by saying: 'the trumpet is the most beautiful sculpture I've ever seen'.

K

kiteminder

We bend our bodies more beautiful beneath the tracings of our memory.

We are ignited.

koto

To travel far as a child is fraught. Boats capsize. Airplanes crash. Bicycles fragment into unusable pieces of metal onto the ground.

The ocean is not an ocean. It is a body of water that meets the land. But it is an ocean. The horses and dogs that run wild on the thin strip of sand before the rocks have permission from the earth. But we too have permission. We too have muscle. Not as strong or as sinewy as the nobler animals but with the same kinetic desires. And so we run, my sister and I, from the gate of our house to the beach while the youngest in our family sleeps within the mosquito net, beneath the fan, the hum of which synthesizes the sounds of chickens and goats coming from the yard outside our house so that this family's youngest, this young boy we call brother, may sleep in good time.

My sister and I run with new muscle that expand and stretch and push our bodies forward. We run in the air that comes from the ocean—that flows over the animals and bids us to carry on. We are as fast as they and soon move among them until I fall and hear the wind and the hammering of hooves against the earth. My uncle runs out and pulls my sister away as the horses run by. He covers her face and looks down the thin strip of sand to see a small explosion of dust where I have fallen. Inside this nebula I am mutilated and bleeding. This was my first death.

SEQUENCE DISRUPTOR 4

dear ms. gla::s,

   i think you fail to understand my predicament but *i show you my leg* has always been my hope. i believe what is needed, and what i have tried to make clear in A-K, is a radical divestment of the values that have hitherto shaped man (the rabbit bunny, the smock of grace jelly, and oodles ohnson eating crispbread in the cabin window). you imply that i have spent my foray into thought lingering on span—that subconscious agenda of salty hypothesis. but i argue that there is a length and breadth to truth that pulls the nipple just right. there is more to the universe than just the pretty girl ms. gla::s. there are the roddy po-po analogies and the ten ways of unhinging fish spit that have a role to play in all of this. there is quicksand and the sustained elevation it would grant our progeny should they be lucky enough to step in it. but I implore you no more letters ms gla::s. send me only kisses if you understand.

undergoing,
s{e}an?

L

luft

in my dream the owl becomes small and then it becomes large again.

Made}line couldn't post such an unloving letter and ordered another coffee, hoping that she would find some loving words to write to poor Regi#na of 362 Marple Ave. After some time passed, she admitted to herself that no loving words were forthcoming. She wasn't sure what she should do. If she could think of no loving words to write to Regi#na, she would try to write loving words to someone else. So she took out a blank sheet of writing paper and put it on the table in front of her and decided to write to Mr. Nort6on Brud^paret of South Livingston Street.

Minutes passed. Still nothing. Then she thought that maybe she was running out of love and that any little love she had left would have to be shared by the seven billion people who lived on this earth. So she wrote a letter with a few loving words and left it on the table for anyone of those seven billion people to find.

Dear seven billion people living on Earth,

I have no more love to give. It's possible that I don't love you like I love some others but that may change. Love is fickle. It's one of those sayings and it's so true. I thought I had more love to give but I don't. So take this little bit that I have left and share it amongst yourselves, if you want it that is. I don't want to force my love on you. That wouldn't be very loving.

Goodbye.

Love (what little I have left for the rest of you),
Made}line

M

memorphacy

swing naught chilly Brutus. The welcome in simple numbers convey. In the doorknob a little sadness goes a long way in making a pretty face. Unload your pistol and bury the universe in my chest.

Everybody wants to forget the day the monsters attacked. When Jasm#ine started ruing the day that she had her palate adjusted. Everybody wondered why she started ruing out of the blue but I knew she was just scared what with all the sun blight and the messenger boy who kept chuckling, one of those nervous chuckles that never calms people down. We were stuck in the lobby for a while before someone came in and told us everything was all right again. But the whole time we were there I kept Jasm#ine calm. I told her everything was going to be okay and that she didn't have to worry about the monsters. I knew they'd be gone soon, or I thought so because I thought to myself, well, after they eat everything there is to eat here, nothing will grow back in time by the time they're hungry again and they'd have to go somewhere else. So I was calm and I guess that made Jasm#ine calm too. She thanked me later. Later that day. But the day after and the day after that and the following week and the following month she just stopped talking to me and kind of disappeared. I'd see her every once in a while though, just like you'd see anybody you didn't know.

N

nuevo-apophenia

rain flowed through the hollow of a fallen bamboo tree and into the river upon which we imagined floating on a giant lotus leaf.

I worry about ants crawling into my ear when I'm lying on the grass. At home there is a pitcher of a green drink on the kitchen table. In the bedroom my brother sets our bed on fire. Outside the window I see Sathan in the empty dirt lot where stray dogs chase each other. I reach into my pocket and wrap my fingers around my airplane. It's still there. Tomorrow at school we will have a fill-in-the-blank test. I will write the word 'blank' for all my answers.

O

order.0

they give us so much to forget.

When I fell in love, I sang about love. I sang about bursting strawberries and globules of thick red strawberries that also burst. I had a passion for (among other things slick and soundproof Chinese harbors) the nobility of man.

Many travel afraid of emptiness. But I am an original thinker and experienced with moments of emptiness (utter and profound).

order.1

we called her flavia and coined her moan.

I can't lean into it and expect listening devices or movements of the Austrian[v] to coincide with my secret tapping. She dances upstairs and [9 portly maidens later] swallows in increments of three, just like loneliness.

SEQUENCE DISRUPTOR 5

dear ms. gla::s,

    sometimes i imagine walking a dog that's not mine and turning down a road toward your house after stopping to watch children drawing with chalk on the sidewalk.

    sometimes i think that you'll knock on my door and i'll look through the window and see you holding up a piece of paper with words written on it that are too small to see.

    there are no symbols here.   nothing means something else. to say i love you means nothing. but to give you all of this means i love you. all of this means one thing. but one thing does not mean all of this.

always sometimes yours,
s{e}an?

P

phonoplane deceleration

oh father would that were ought a man so conceived as thee to thine maker's eye, but savage nature upon thee has thrust its brazen stare. Oh cold hand.

Penelope blamed herself for much that was wrong with the world. When there was a fire it was because she hadn't eaten from each food group on that particular day. If a murder took place it was because she thought too long about buying a new pair of shoes when she didn't really need them. She spent her young life trying to figure out how she could stop bad things from happening but she was always doing something to bring down all the goodness of the world. Every once in a while she didn't care. She just let herself go: an assault, a rape, mass starvation. She felt that it was beyond her control to care all the time because caring all the time was inhuman.

propeller

the death of the mule reached mar(w)in. A bur like string and the word 'the' saw the sun, a piece of black skin, and orange rinds for geppeto. Under the love blanch, the criminy chronicles ferment. Love baby, love.

And so the little boy half-asleep with a small white cloth wrapped around his head and tubes coming from underneath reached his arm from beneath (his blanket) to touch the woman's face. He mumbled something to her that she didn't understand and touched her chin. With her hand, she followed his. From her chin to her cheek. From her cheek to her hair, which he grasped at as if he were searching for something in the darkness.

The woman leaned closer to him but gave his hand the space it needed to wander. Searching and searching until he found the yellow barrette decorated with red and purple flowers that kept her face opened to him. She unclasped the barrette and put it in his palm. He closed his fingers around it and turned onto his side.

"Close your eyes", the woman said.

She caressed his head.

The boy looked at her reflection in the window and said: "we do not want to close our eyes".

Q

quicknesses[vi]

i should set sail these creatures to placid shorebrows and make amends for the dalliance of my uterus.

It's like one of those Pas‖cal cube things that's a part of life without people realizing it. I choose the second choice, which is like the musical note C. I remember it from school. Not like they remember, because they don't remember. They just forget. They forget because they all speak the same way and it's hard to remember people who don't speak the same way because people think you have a communication problem and never start listening when it's only that you say things a little bit differently. Like strawbaby for example and all that other stuff I can't quite picture but I know is right there (there…when the sun shines on your face or you're sitting too close to the light). But Pas‖cal was my favorite composer because he used a lot of rodondos and fermatas.

SEQUENCE DISRUPTOR 6

dearest s{e}an?,

we are but foot soldiers in the march of our blood. and in our blood i dream of us across the prairie grass where we paint a trail for our kind to follow.

all things i give, i give to you,
e{m}ma+

R

rememory

starting with the trees. Starting with the path leading to the trees. The trees were tall in the forest. She turned to look back. Slowly mon ami. And the leaves? They fell did they not? So many. So many fell around her. And then she turned again. Slowly. My god she turned. So slowly, so full of grace, that we mistook her for air.

It's no small feat to make one's way. It requires an understanding of the metaphysics between one's self and the objects that orbit one's self. It would have been no surprise to Molly and her objugates if she had awakened one morning and wished for a kind of normal that comes without explanations. But Molly's normal came with an urgent request for the revolver. She fitted herself and boosted, earmarking destinations little by little and quite by...she and she and she...

The pagoda before her bustled with reference. The least of which, the pole, who left because of the girl who loved, like so, ever so, in fact, just so. For if we give Molly the revolver, she will take it apart and rebuild the universe.

And not so simple many subjects *harrowed* she lay in bed. And did this for many minutes. So many, in fact, that calling them minutes would understate the many-ness of them. Through the space between the curtain and the window she saw yarn (a dusty equivalent of rain). Maybe she'd cross her eyes and fall back to sleep. She was pretty.

And [lo] there on her pillow a capsule shaped amoeba. Brackish and then finally the. A balmy thing she held between erstwhile blah blah blah and tiger lily bleh bleh bleh. But she'll make her way as the laid goat is ambulatory and able to suffice the pristine and scrumptious.

There is, after all, no limit to one's willy-nilly.

It was now that Molly read the letter. But in a parastasis of saidbefores, no one writes letters any, uhm, longer. Not f. Or y. Or a consonant reacclimation of the punjabi, which had a sheen, thoughtful and unencumbered but was still [sidebar your honor] like this.

Bring me the burlap cockles Thurston.

Should Molly sit by the fire and listen to the violin while her homonym relishes different states of undress, philosophers will go through her drawers and search for truth in her lower vowels. They'll find it and foretell events of one who entered for the implixic..imploaxic...implamative purpose of dropping the revolver. Right there. There. Over there. For her to see.

Here is an overview of the palisade. Please remember the date.

One surmises that the purpose of her visit is twofold:

1. to teach us how to dance on mud

2. so far and like pummel

Perhaps one surmised correctly but one can't be sure of what one can't be certain of. And...processing...I left the revolver by her side. As

I walked away, boodle kitswinny erupted and the [then the] sting of such failure [instinctual].

Oh ache. Oh longing. Oh darn it.

Molly knew more than anyone that beauty was painful. To see it, heartbreaking. So much so [much so [much so]] that she would collapse in a heap and cry uncontrollably. And when she couldn't for reasons "behind her sorrow" she clenched her jaw, jiggled in acknowledgment, and mumbled god save the queen. But she happily served the greatest and least seen tyrant of them all.

It was here that "Sad Molly the pingo" was introduced not for the benefit of humanity but for its definitive destruction. What happened to sad the pingo remains a mystery to this day. But Molly lay on the bed with the revolver. Before she started taking it apart she moved the blanket to reveal her leg [pantyfruit]. What a gorgeous plot of scrubby! First the barrel. Then the spring action telemetry. When she removed the firing pin the left side of my face fell to the floor. By the time she had the revolver in pieces strewn about the bed I was the second toe of my right foot.

Enter Cassius--

Shall I make a memory of thine fissure and strike at the breast of merriment? Oh noble chameleon of many coloured hues, tinges, and shades. Yonder.

S

sendmatter

the wind through your spine whistles my favorite tune. Meet me at extinction. The airport is accessible by throat.

Mol..ly visited today. I became her. I sensed that she felt in me a brief awakening to the image framed by the window. She pulled the curtains further apart. I thought if she and I were together out there, standing by the tree, and someone not so unlike me watched from this very room, that this watcher would be evil and succumb to one of the many evils known to man. Perhaps the evil of knifing and the slitting that is an integral part of it.

submatter

during the procedure we discovered that her dark humors failed to mutate, leading to the inoperable metabolizing of her bilirubin.

It's not easy to end your feelings in a good way even when you're alone. It all starts off okay. You feel angry or sad or happy but then there's a knock on your door or your fish die and even when they don't there's always that threat hanging over you, so you end up worrying about the fish dying or somebody walking in on you while you're in the middle of feeling perplexed or in the middle of some other feeling. The butterflies did that to me. I knew they would come back but I didn't want anyone else to know. So I ran away from home. I ran as fast I could but they were everywhere. They knocked me to the ground and I figured I'd just lie on my belly and cover my head and wait until they all disappeared but they started pummeling me. I tried to fight back but then I thought maybe they would pummel me so much that they would change the shape and look of my face and in between pummels they would realize they were pummeling the wrong person. So I stopped fighting them and I just let them pummel me. When they finished pummeling me I went home and asked my mother if there was anything about my face that had changed. She said she couldn't really see anything different. Except for all that blood and petrol albumin.

SEQUENCE DISRUPTOR 7

dearest e{m}ma+,

   i move according to my needs and circumvent rationalizations in order to get straight to the heart of the matter. i remember the ribald scatter of desde!mona's skirt in the hilly wind and how it shaded the olive grass. but finally and to my derision how unloved the one-horned pink surfaced two trees between bark and (unseen). who will brush our teeth when we're gone? dearest e{m}ma. i remember your name carved on a blade of grass and laundered another memory to deposit there as you and me. it grows. but what of it? it lessens zilch. it travels. it eschews and brands ram tartar and sully swingfree and pecuniary on the picnic blanket. e{m}ma+, that's my knee and manly chinbone. it's no one else's and i give it all to you.

   in the house we hear noises and i say: "they mean harm."

   and you say: "who?"

   and i say: "there is a causal arousal between your twinge and the tall ships that boing water. like dummies they'll sproing later. and in a drama, make that loiter, they'll poing after."

   but it's not daring to wonder how bland the human mind (is), unable to move between ticks and drum processions. for summer we'll be lovers and listen to someone named ca=rm//en espino)(za scorch cabaret in the bubble lounge.

my arm is covered in skin and reaches out to you,

s{e}an?

T

testaments betrothed

you destroy, i create, i destroy

Steadfast in our belief that what we reach for is not far—the temple organism, Paler and Granite[vii], drown in their own poison (and whisper "our cause of death is drowning"). What we find here is not so different from the likes of order if there is order.

.

U

universe of dust

*she answers the prefect with a gam, parallel to the
floor and adoring. Such a perfect kneecap. And the
sheen of her inner thigh. That's a five-blade ceiling
fan my child. Then the precious niblet. She doesn't
offer the traditional rebellion. Hers is subtle and
more difficult to engage.*

The boy doesn't know any better right now. He
only knows he wants something. So when he sees
the flower growing from the shoe he walks over to
the shoe and pulls the flower out. Then he runs off
and sits under a table with it. He scatters the petals
and the stem on the floor around him then runs back
to the shoe for another flower. But there are no
more flowers in the shoe and that puzzles him.

V

VILE AGAINST THE NEW WORLD

sentence against the pathological consistency of a predetermined civilization

If on Friday her pounce has been misidentified, reparations will be made, but until then we shall sit and wait and ponder the indemnity of such deeds soberly and without retrenchment, so sympathetic and in such tender rain my closet dalliance with the Austrian, who waltzed by herself—and the cheetah—in the room above made known to the world at large, died by herself, her death compounded by an intractable will, condemned to whisper her last words to me while three moments passed, as her lips reached my ear, two recognized, one found in my Dictionary of Coincidences[viii], but none the girl Chinese and uninvolved, who spit tea as she drove by Stockholm Central Station, her cabin window reflecting the roof lights and the snow outlined by dusk as it ascended the carriage track, penultimate and foreboding, three Latin words reconfigured by the foreigner standing in the doorway of the architect Joseph who, unknown to me, smiled a knowing smile and waved to his children fare thee well (bye bye), all the while resisting the partition, the letter s, the letter f, the subterranean flicker alone between two cheeks and distended jaw bone, a thin whisper (when he whispered) of the jackass on the hill, the present-leg

113

elephant beak fractured for posebee and the formal restitution of the dark gender, its cushion whip drafting blood to practice aryan intuition, two boodles slit and a fiddle of skinbow laid down softly by iron from the town that intervenes trainstops where fenwich and brood and i can't remember sink fishbrawn for kicks and naked ruddernips, two graves down from a murderous intention but not today nor tomorrow (shall they) jump ship the sail or flay Portuguese castanets for the funeral procession of the great man who, when asked the simple question how are you replied "never again".

W

warling

what has damaged these creatures of an ominous but weak nature, teeth bent to imitate bite—the dumb animal? And how could such a mistake forge such finery, from pockmarked faces and philistine hues stretched to invisible, those splendid flowers they place to die upon their graves?

dear momma,

its been a long time since I have writen but I want you and everyone to know that I am all rite here. Everbodys' been wonderfull and last nite I had vanila ice cream for desert. I brouht my robe with me on acount that you told me it woud rase my self asteem if I walkt round in it and pretented I was a vanpire or somethin cos of montsers bein' afraid of other montsers in the dark and if'n I was a montser then there ain't nothin to be afraid of in the dark. It was just like you said momma. Ain't nobdy even messin with me and I'm warin the robe all off the time now even when I'm outside and doin work. They try to make me not ware it but they ain't got no rules about what I can ware here and I hippotize them any ole way and now they all walkin round like gohstes.

115

X

xiblet

*i wondered if it was a feeling i could change or if
the feeling would change on its own.*

While travelling to the new world, Purdy wrote a
play entitled "Giblet". He directed passengers and
members of the crew in a staging of "Giblet" on the
ship somewhere in the middle of the Atlantic
Ocean. The cast had difficulty reading his writing as
he came to reveal that he had one finger missing on
his writing hand. But after much frustration and
direction, Giblet was performed to a standing only
crowd. Captain Robtre played the role of Giblet.
Mrs. Evelynne Jame of Black Fryers played
Cassandra.

*Captain Robtre & Mrs. Evelynne Jame of Black
Fryars as drawn by Purdy*

Y

you can stop if you want to

perhaps I had other desires before this one but I can't remember them. I will take the airplane to school and push it across my desk while the teacher talks about subtraction.

This work has come to an end. What follows is an analysis of this work. From the beginning what is known as the prologue to the end about me. I captured ideas throughout this work that were of a hidden or complacent nature. Unlike electron particles constantly in movement they were motionless. Still. And though I have conspired to significantly alter that which has existed for millions of years, I have failed. This failure is evident throughout this work. And yet, in this failure, a filament exists that brings pleasure to the soul-less writer. It is true. The writer has no soul. What is perceived as soul is only a misunderstanding of the longing for physical contact and the grinding, sociopathic disinclinations of the isolated.

yyyyy

i know elephants. I know that if Nostalgia and I meet in the elephant then it's meant to be. And if we don't, we'll accept it and move on. So we won't time our entrance. We'll just do what we do and kick this rock as we walk because we love country roads. We think we know what they look like.

We run with others in the cold, our winter hats coming loose from our heads, then falling off. We should find them before we go home. Our parents will be angry that we have lost them. We shouldn't run like this but there is no other way to fight this evil. We stay in motion. We move and spit. We roll on the ground and give up our skin to the cold gravel—little pieces scraped off by the rough, infinitesimal blots of blood injected into the ruts. I think that one day something will walk through this space, lean down, and place the tip of its tongue on the microscopic remnants of skin and blood we have left behind.

Z

zebra horse

i have a drop slip katy moffit urge.

My favourite river has always been the Mekong. Cars park there and people kiss. Sometimes strangers stand beside each other and look into the water as tachybaptus ruficollis watch them from above.

SEQUENCE DISRUPTOR 8

dear s{e}an?,

    when we are old we must save play for the young. surrender it in shame and in shame accept their ridicule. we must walk the garden of serpents and feel their animal blood in our spine. we must go blind and die before we reach the end. that is our end. who would be reproached for thinking that such a creature could ever inspire awe? and yet *we* are awed. here in our face, tall ships cross the sea and descend into the vitreous.

(love always (love always (love always,
e{m}ma+

The Epilogue

from the Arch-Enemies Handbook

It is with good intentions that I wish for everyone an arch-enemy. But not everyone is predisposed *to* or capable *of* living with an arch-enemy. "living with" as in existing on the same planet at the same time. Arch-enemies can be imagined and/or non-reciprocating. These types of arch-enemies, however, do not allow us to develop the powers necessary for combating our real arch-enemies. Imagined or non-reciprocating arch-enemies are good practice but everyone (in good time) needs the power of a real arch-enemy to endure and eventually overcome.

It was in second grade that I developed my first real arch-enemy: Sathan. It was this relationship that provided the arc and structure of my subsequent arch-enemy relationships.

Sathan and I were good friends at the beginning of the school year but by the third quarter, due to some real or perceived injustice (any slight will do), we had become true and committed arch-enemies. A good friend is the best candidate for a future arch-enemy and by becoming one and opposing you, bestows upon you the greatest honour any friend ever could.

about s{e}an?

[itfu esd nptm om ejsy od mpe rmh;smf voyu rmh;smf jod gsyjrt esd s ytsfrt om rsdyrtm d[ovrd/ jod ,pyjrt esd s domhrt om yjr vpity pg rst; [omwipy/ jod rst;u urstd ertr d[rmy ytsbr;;omh eoyj jod gsyjrt sd gst rsdy sd ,pmkp;os smf sd gst mptyj sd ;s[;smf/ om jod yrrmd jr [;surf yjr jst[smf drtbrf sd s nsvl=i[domhrt gpt jod ,pyjrt

D ypitomh ,omdytr: htpi[/ jod [rtgpt,omh fsud. Pert. Vs,r yp sm rmf sgyrt s jsmf svvofrmy/ sy yjr shr pg yermyu yjtrr jr ;rgy jp,r pm s djo[npimf gpt yjr mre in writing, as in all other forms of art, the spectator is irrelevant to the true purpose of art. For the true purpose of art is to increase the power of the creator—to elevate the creator, if only for a moment, above the mediocrity of man and in so doing elevate all of mankind above itself. It is in the *disjecta membra* of this process that those who choose not to create see any value in art—the creation of something beautiful, the illusion of meaning, the revelation of the many possibilities of existence...

lovenotes

[i]Gaston Ribera, former waiter and boyfriend of Maria who drowned herself in the ocean, under a palm tree. Oranges and leaves.

[ii]A graphical representation of the Lily Analysis.

[iii]A seaside locality in Kungälv Municipality, Västra Götaland County, Sweden

[iv]I don't know what happens to the butterflies. I can't find any news about them. So I'm thinking about getting on my bicycle and maybe taking a journey somewhere to find them. Those things head for the sun or they go in the opposite direction.

[v]Last night I wrote about my day (July 17, 2023) in my diary. I used a sturdy stylus pen with a brushed satin-chrome barrel and rubberized grip. That was neat. I embellished one or two of the day's events for the purposes of posterity, but who will ever know? I also drew a picture of a naked woman in the margin and made one of her nipples bigger than the other. That made me smile. After I looked at the picture a little bit, I colored over it with a thick, black magic marker that I took from a cup on my desk. And then I closed my diary and put it in the drawer. That's all for today.

[vi]Like quicknesses.

[vii]When I was a boy I had a crabdog. Although I shouldn't say 'had' because he didn't really belong

to me. He didn't belong to anybody. One day—I remember it like it was today—I took his claw carefully in my hand and we walked to the woods together. I whistled a tune and crabdog wagged his tail. We lay down in an opening in the forest and looked up to the clouds through the trees. I told crabdog that one of the clouds looked like him. He jumped up and down, snapping his claws at the leaves and branches hanging above us. I pulled crabdog under my arm and fell asleep. When I woke up I saw that crabdog was gone and that one of my fingers was missing. There was a lot of blood. But I couldn't be angry at crabdog. It was just an instinct for him. I yelled out for him—to let him know that it was okay. But I didn't see any sign of him. I looked up to the sky as if someone or something could help me, when I saw the clouds take the form of crabdog. My soul shuddered and a giant tear hung from the corner of my eye.

[viii]e{m}ma+ gla::s